Copyright © 2016 by Immaginare Press

All rights reserved. No part of this book may be reproduced in any form without written permission from the publisher.

Library of Congress Cataloging in Publication Data available.

ISBN: 978-1-941677-31-5

Printed in China

Immaginare Press
1200 Chickory Lane
Los Angeles, CA 90049

immaginarepress.com

Print management by Burnett Print Group, LLC, Burbank, CA

In 1781 Los Angeles came to be. The Spanish named the city "El Pueblo de Nuestra Senora la Reina de Los Angeles", translated, The Town of Our Lady, the Queen of the Angels of the Porciuncula River." After Los Angeles had changed hands from Spain to Mexico, the town was officially declared a city in 1835 becoming part of the United States in 1847. Los Angeles is spread out over a large, diverse metropolis.

The city sits in a basin, surrounded by the San Gabriel Mountain range and divided by the Santa Monica Mountains. Los Angeles County has miles of picturesque coastline, with some of the greatest beaches and surf spots. With museums, exhibits, and street art, Los Angeles is a perfect place to experience the dramatic skylines while exploring the intriguing art and culture of the city.

The Vincent Thomas Bridge is a 1,500-foot-long suspension bridge, crossing the Los Angeles Harbor linking San Pedro with Terminal Island. Opened in 1963. June · 8:08 PM

Eastern Columbia Building is a unique art deco building located in the Broadway Theatre and historical district. Designed by architect Claud Beelman in 1930.

October · 7:08 PM

October · 7:16 AM

← Pasadena Freeway, October · 6:04 PM | On the Train, October · 7:32 PM

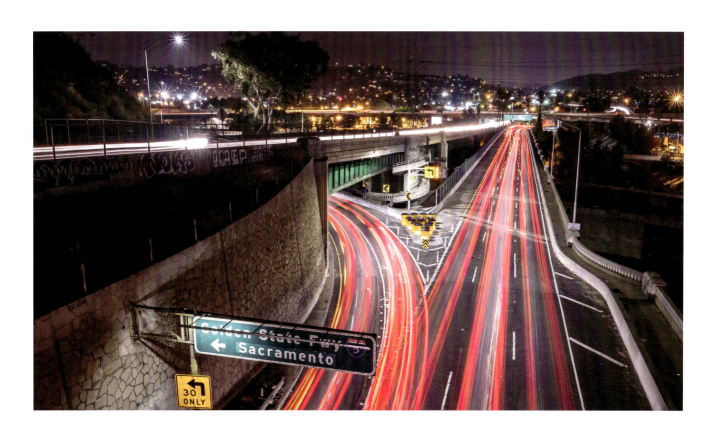

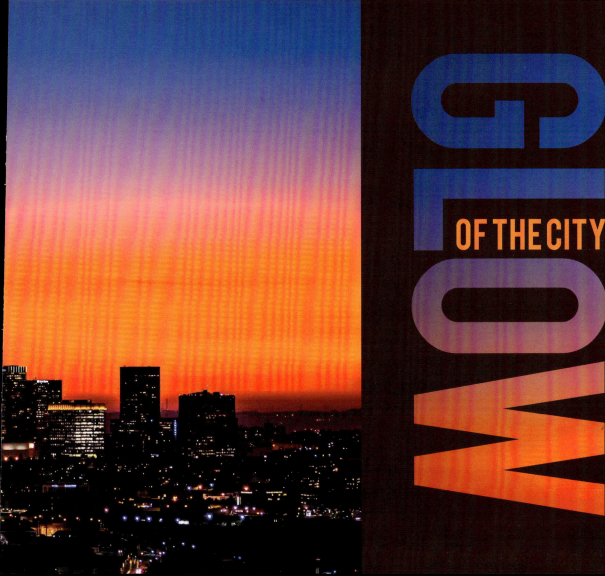

October · 7:21 AM

Sunset over the top of Amalfi, Pacific Palisades. October · 6:06 PM

LA
SUNSET

From the Griffith Park Observatory · December · 6:33 AM

February · 7:48 AM

Arthur J. Will Memorial Fountain at City Hall.

NOBODY WALKS IN LA

Upper: September · 9:18 PM | Lower: August · 6:45 PM

Dorothy Chandler Pavilion

Sunrise photo from the hills above the Getty. December · 6:50 AM

Overlooking Santa Monica Bay   December · 5:05 PM

All: December · 4:48 to 5:12 PM

Skyline over the Hollywood Bowl. June · 7:31 PM

SKYLINE

September · 6:03 AM

Above the Hollywood sign.   October · 5:37 AM

September · 5:42 AM

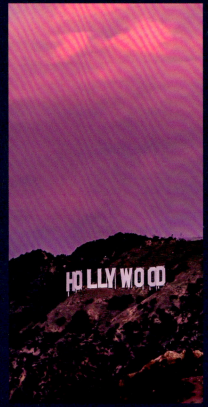
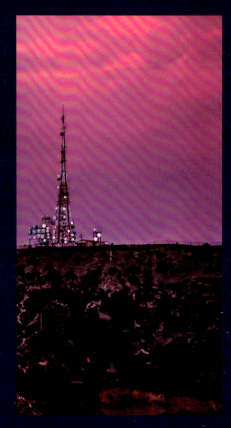

October · 6:10 AM

Above the Griffith Park Observatory looking out to downtown. Located in the hills of Griffith Park just above the Los Feliz neighborhood, Griffith Observatory has been a Los Angeles icon since 1935.

CITY OF ANGELS

SERENITY

August · 4:00 PM

December · 6:35 AM

December · 7:10 AM

Above, July · 1:17 AM | Below, March · 5:46 AM

USC Parking Lot · September · 5:49 AM

Orpheum Theatre on Broadway, LA, opened in 1926.   June · 8.07 PM

The 2nd Street Tunnel. This is a famous tunnel used in many movies. It sits under Bunker Hill in Downtown LA

An early morning on Broadway walking past the Orpheum Theatre   October · 6:57 AM

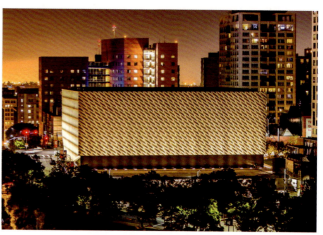

Disney Hall and The Broad Museum

Disney Hall · February · 8.34 AM

City Hall. March · 4:44 PM

Union Station · January · 10:59 PM

October · 5:39 AM

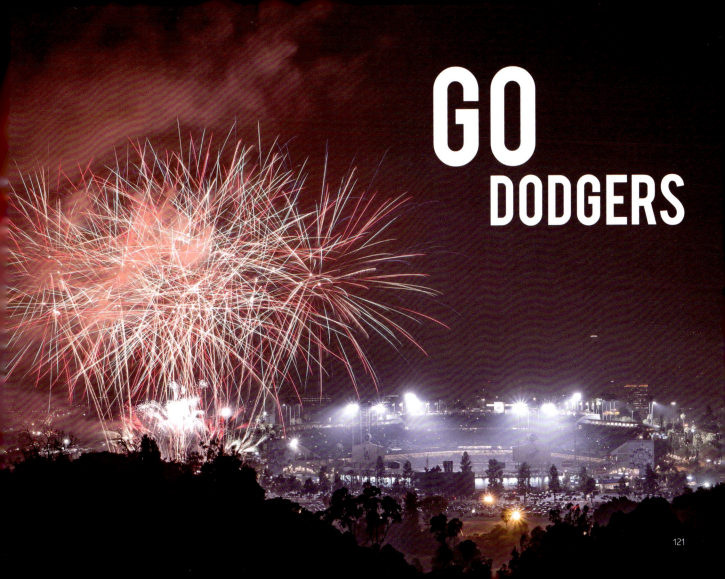

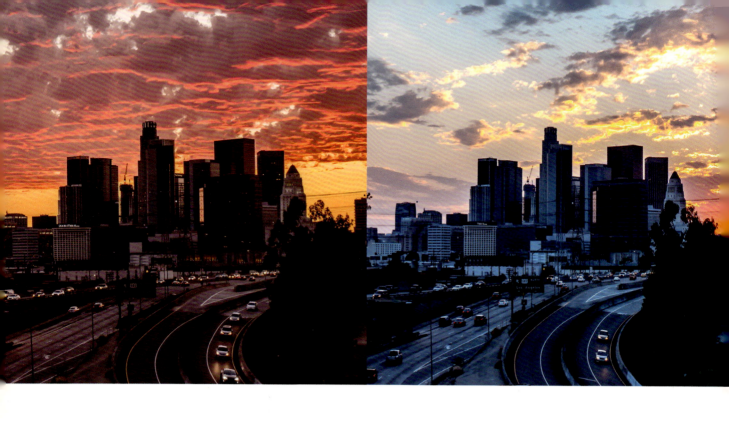

Hollywood Freeway to the Harbor Freeway

6th Street Bridge. September · 6:04 PM

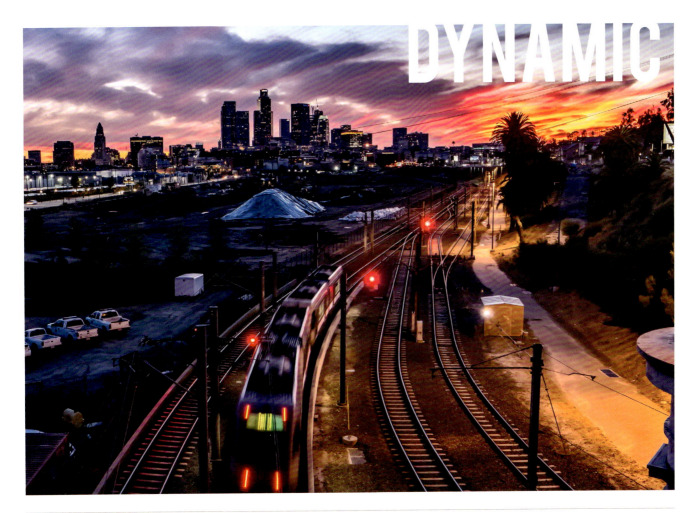

LA River with 6th Street bridge (demolished in Feb 2016). 9.30 PM

Los Angeles Theatre located on Broadway was constructed in 1930.

ECHO PARK

Below, left: The Chandelier Tree in Silverlake.

View from Hollywood Bowl overlook.   June · 8:16 PM

December · 6:36 PM

View above the pool at Yamashiro Restaurant. December · 8:01 PM

Downtown LA Hill Street. March · 6:40 PM

The historical United Artist Theater building, 1927. Converted to The Ace Hotel in 2014.

Capitol Records

Hollywood and Vine.

Christmas Day · December · 4:46 PM

Clouds over the Pacific   May · 3:07 PM

Looking to downtown and the San Gabriel Mountains. April · 6:00 AM

A perfect day looking at the J. Paul Getty to downtown.   February · 4:19 PM

January · 6:30 AM

View over West LA to Los Angeles Harbor · May · 3:36 PM

Taken from above the Hollywood sign.   September · 6:49 AM

SPRING

November · 6:17 PM

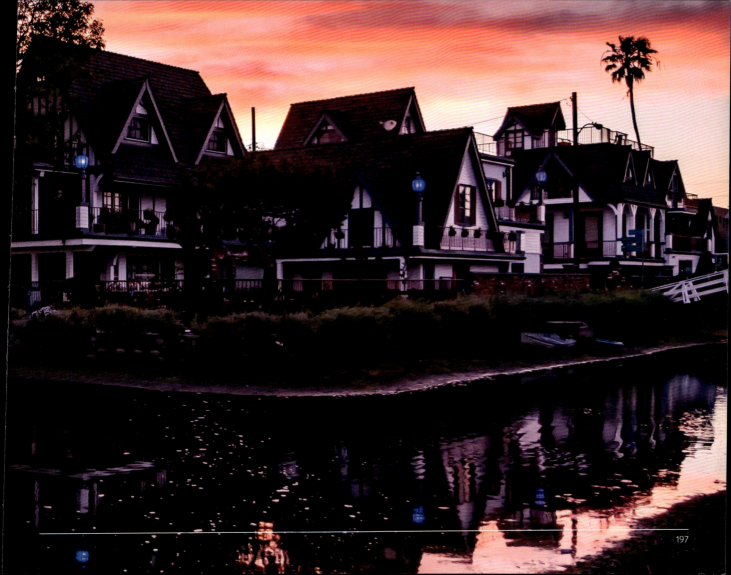

Venice Canals sunset – March 6.13 – 6:19 PM

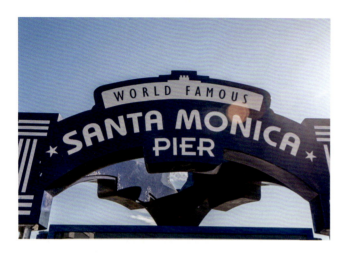

SANTA MONICA

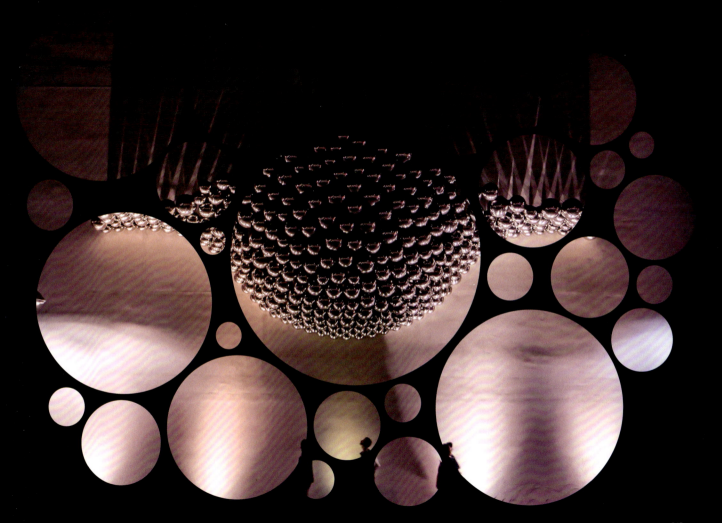

Malibu Sunset. October · 6:05 PM

Salomon Peña
Photographer

Salomon's patience and discipline developed during his years in the US Marine Corps. He now focuses his attention-to-detail through his camera lens. Armed with his trusty Panasonic GH 4 and a few energy bars, Salomon is out scouting for locations long before most Angelenos are even awake. He is constantly seeking a unique aspect to capture his native Los Angeles.

Dain Blair
Photographer

Dain Blair's career covers everything from playing guitar and bass in touring bands, working with Capitol Records to heading up custom music house, Grooveworx. Dain has always been captivated by scenic views and water from his childhood years spent in the Panama Canal Zone between the Pacific and Atlantic Oceans. He enjoys capturing sunrises, sunsets, and oceans and whenever possible both simultaneously. He is always on the look out for a sky more impressive than the last. His passion has steered him all over the world. Dain's work is featured in 'Los Angeles, sunrise to sunset,' 'Ocean' and 'The Beach Umbrella.'

Saloman Peña

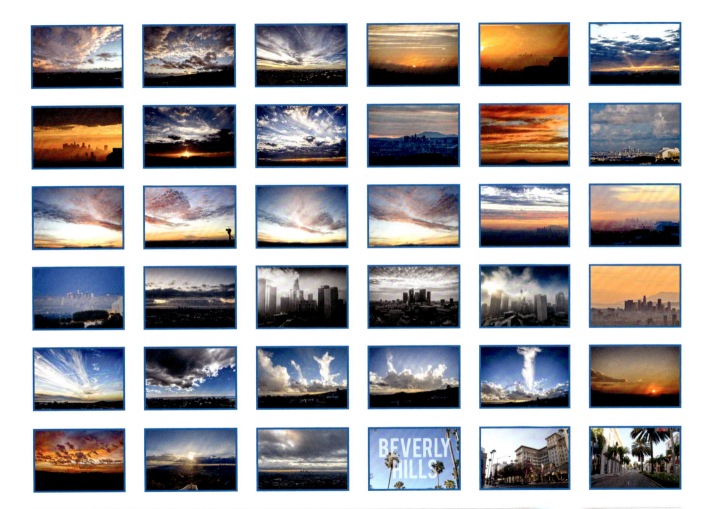

Dain Blair

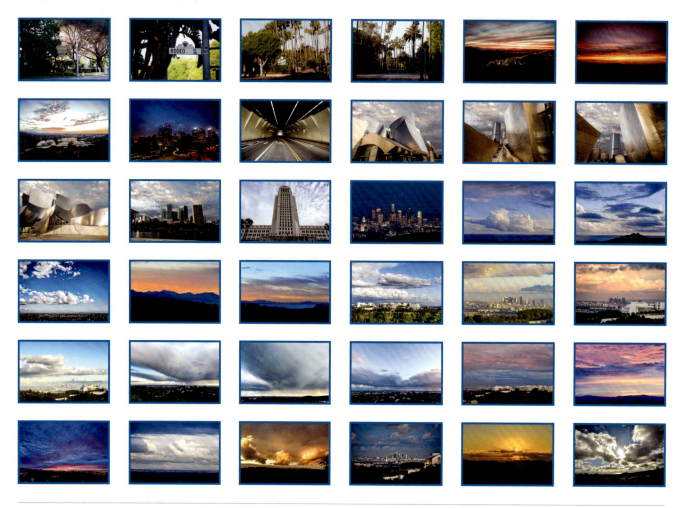

Dain Blair